Movement
of PEOPLE

REFUGEES & DISPLACEMENT

BY
SHALINI VALLEPUR

BookLife
PUBLISHING

©2021
BookLife Publishing Ltd.
King's Lynn
Norfolk PE30 4LS

ISBN: 978-1-83927-165-6

Written by:
Shalini Vallepur

Edited by:
Madeline Tyler

Designed by:
Drue Rintoul

CONTENTS

WORDS THAT LOOK LIKE <u>THIS</u> ARE EXPLAINED IN THE GLOSSARY ON PAGE 31.

THE MOVEMENT OF PEOPLE

Take a look at the world around you. How many ships cross the ocean every day? How many lorries come in and out of different countries? Throughout time, people have moved around the planet, creating new countries and building new homes. They have explored, traded and even fought with other people from across the world. Our world is shaped by the movement of people.

IT DOESN'T MATTER WHO YOU ARE OR WHERE YOU ARE FROM — ANYBODY CAN MIGRATE, AND DIFFERENT PEOPLE MIGRATE FOR DIFFERENT REASONS.

Our world is never still. People have always wanted to explore and move around the planet and will continue to do so for years to come. We are able to share so many things with each other because of the movement of people; from food and movies to festivals and books, our world is becoming smaller and most people are free to enjoy the world. However, some people have also been made to move when they didn't want to. How does this affect the world? And how is the movement of people between different countries controlled?

WHY MOVE?

People travel for lots of different reasons. Some people travel to a new country because they have a new job, and some people might travel to find a safe place to live. There are different reasons for why people move around or leave their home country to find a new place to live. These reasons are sometimes called push and pull factors. Think about it this way: what things might push somebody to leave their home, and what things might pull them to a new one and mean it's a better place to live?

PUSH FACTORS

- NOT ENOUGH JOBS
- <u>PERSECUTION</u>
- LACK OF SAFETY
- WAR
- <u>NATURAL DISASTERS</u>
- <u>FAMINE</u>

PULL FACTORS

- MORE JOB OPPORTUNITIES
- FREEDOM FROM PERSECUTION
- SAFETY AND SECURITY
- BETTER EDUCATION OPPORTUNITIES
- BETTER HEALTHCARE
- CLOSER TO FAMILY

WHO'S WHO?

Migration means movement. There are lots of different words that you might hear to describe the <u>status</u> of people who migrate. Here are a few to help you understand.

REFUGEE: a person who has been forced to leave their home country or an asylum seeker who has been given permission to stay in another country

ASYLUM SEEKER: a refugee who has left their home country and has applied for safety, or <u>asylum</u>, in another country

RESETTLED: when an asylum seeker has travelled to a different country, been recognised as a refugee and sent to a second country to live <u>permanently</u>

DISPLACED: a person who has been forced to leave their usual home

INTERNALLY DISPLACED: a person who has been forced to leave their usual home and is still in their home country and is not considered a refugee

IMMIGRANT: a person who comes to live in a new country permanently, usually for work

ASYLUM SEEKERS AND REFUGEES

The terms 'asylum seeker' and 'refugee' can be difficult to understand. Let's take a look at where these terms come from and explore what they mean.

HUMAN RIGHTS AND THE REFUGEE CONVENTION

In 1948, after World War Two, the UN put together a document called the Universal Declaration of Human Rights. The document gave every single human being basic rights, such as the right to vote, the right to live safely and the right to go to school. These rights allow all people to live freely and safely. In 1951, the Refugee Convention added to these rights and further defined what it meant to be a refugee or asylum seeker. The countries that are part of the UN must follow and support the human rights of all people, even the people in countries that aren't part of the UN.

BY THE END OF WORLD WAR TWO, IT IS THOUGHT THAT BETWEEN 7 AND 11 MILLION DISPLACED PEOPLE WERE LIVING IN GERMANY, ITALY AND AUSTRIA. THE NEW ACTS AND LAWS WERE PUT IN PLACE TO PROTECT ALL PEOPLE.

REFUGEES

The 1951 Refugee Convention says a refugee is a person who is outside their home country and is unable or unwilling to return due to a well-founded fear of persecution. In most cases, refugees don't want to leave their homes but are forced to because their lives are in danger. Sometimes, a refugee is also a person who has left their home and applied for and been given asylum by another country. When somebody has been given refugee status, they are allowed to stay in the new country for a set amount of time. Refugees can stay in the UK for five years. After five years, they can either apply to stay in the UK permanently, or return to their home country if it is safe to do so.

MANY PEOPLE WERE PERSECUTED AND KILLED DURING WORLD WAR TWO FOR THEIR BELIEFS.

ASYLUM SEEKERS

An asylum seeker is a person, or refugee, who has been forced to leave their home country and has applied for asylum in another country. The Human Rights Act says that every single person has the right to seek asylum, or look for a safe place to live. When an asylum seeker gets to a new country, they must claim asylum from the government of that country. Usually the asylum seeker must tell the government what happened to them and why they are afraid of going back to their home. An asylum seeker is allowed to stay in that country while they are waiting for the government to make a decision.

SEEKING ASYLUM MEANS LOOKING FOR A SAFE PLACE TO LIVE.

MIGRANTS

A migrant is a person who has chosen to leave their home country and move to another country. A person may move because they are looking for a new job, going to a new school or looking to live closer to other family members. They do not leave their home country because they are in danger and they can usually return to their home country safely. This is different for refugees and asylum seekers, whose lives are at risk if they are made to return to their home country.

THE TERMS ASYLUM SEEKER, REFUGEE AND MIGRANT ARE SOMETIMES USED IN PLACE OF ONE ANOTHER. SOMETIMES A PERSON MIGHT NOT FIT ANY OF THESE WORDS. IT'S IMPORTANT TO ALWAYS THINK ABOUT THE PERSON BEHIND THE TERM AND WHAT THEY HAVE BEEN THROUGH.

PUSHED TO MOVE

L et's take a look at some of the push factors that might force a person to leave their home.

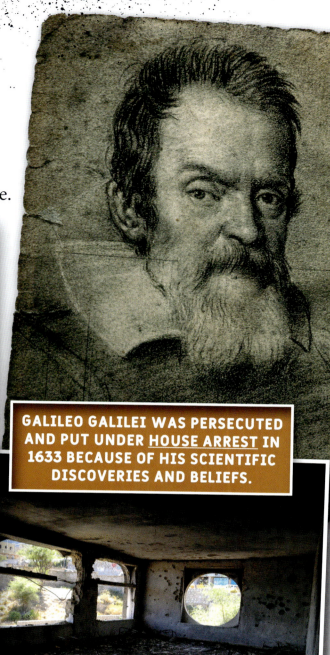

WHAT IS PERSECUTION?

The fear of persecution is the main reason that people become refugees, but what exactly does this mean? Persecution usually happens when a person's human rights have been <u>violated</u> and they are not able to live freely or safely. This usually means a person is being treated badly because of their religion, nationality, the things they believe in, or what they look like. People can be persecuted in different ways. Everybody has the right to follow a religion but some people are persecuted for their religious beliefs by being put in prison. Sometimes persecution can be extremely violent as people can be <u>tortured</u> or even killed because of who they are. When large groups of people face persecution, they have no choice but to leave where they are.

GALILEO GALILEI WAS PERSECUTED AND PUT UNDER <u>HOUSE ARREST</u> IN 1633 BECAUSE OF HIS SCIENTIFIC DISCOVERIES AND BELIEFS.

WHEN HOSPITALS AND OTHER PUBLIC BUILDINGS ARE DESTROYED, PEOPLE ARE FORCED TO FIND HELP ELSEWHERE.

WARS

War and fighting often forces people to leave their homes. Weapons such as bombs are often used during wars. Bombs can destroy people's homes, schools and other important buildings. This can force people to search for a safe place for themselves and their families. Areas that aren't directly bombed or targeted are still badly affected by war and fighting. The <u>infrastructure</u> in a country may be damaged and governments may not be able to support everyone, making life for ordinary people difficult or even impossible. During a war, there might be no access to food, water, medicine or education. When basic things are lost, the risk of famine or disease increases and people's lives are put in danger. This forces people to leave their homes.

NATURAL DISASTERS

Natural disasters such as hurricanes, earthquakes, tsunamis and forest fires often force people out of their homes. Natural disasters can destroy the infrastructure of cities and towns as well as buildings and people's homes. This forces people to move from their homes and look for safety somewhere else.

BECOMING A REFUGEE

These are just a few of the ways that a person can be forced into becoming a refugee or asylum seeker. Many people can become refugees for other reasons. It is important to understand that nobody wants to be a refugee or asylum seeker. Most people become a refugee or asylum seeker because they don't have a choice and they must protect themselves and their families.

THE VIETNAM WAR

The Vietnam War saw many Vietnamese refugees seeking safety, but how did this happen and what forced people to move?

The Vietnam War was fought between 1955 and 1973. In 1954, Vietnam was split into two areas – North Vietnam and South Vietnam. North and South Vietnam had very different political systems and controlled their areas and people in very different ways. North Vietnam wanted to join together with South Vietnam and make everybody follow their way of life. This, along with other reasons, led to the Vietnam War.

NORTH VIETNAM

Armies from North Vietnam began to fight the armies of South Vietnam. Some countries, such as the US, feared that North Vietnam's political system would spread to South Vietnam, the rest of Asia and eventually the world. This led to the US fighting alongside the armies of South Vietnam, against North Vietnam.

SOUTH VIETNAM

POWERFUL PEOPLE AND GOVERNMENTS SOMETIMES USE WAR AND FIGHTING TO FORCE PEOPLE TO FOLLOW WHAT THEY BELIEVE IS RIGHT. ORDINARY PEOPLE ARE OFTEN CAUGHT IN THE FIGHTING AND SUFFER.

BOMBS AND HERBICIDES

The US Army fought the Viet Cong - supporters of North Vietnam - in South Vietnam. They used bombs to destroy towns and villages that the Viet Cong were hiding in, but many innocent Vietnamese people were caught in the bombing. <u>Herbicides</u> were used to destroy trees and plants so that the Viet Cong couldn't hide in forests. While the herbicides destroyed forests, they also destroyed farms and crops, leaving many people with little to eat. The destruction and damage caused by the fighting meant that many ordinary Vietnamese people were in danger.

THE HERBICIDES CAUSED TERRIBLE INJURIES TO VIETNAMESE AND AMERICAN PEOPLE AND SOME PEOPLE ARE STILL AFFECTED BY THE HERBICIDES TODAY.

PERSECUTION

In 1975, North Vietnam took control of the city of Saigon in South Vietnam. This joined the two areas together to make Vietnam. Many people believed this was the end of the war but many Vietnamese people were still treated badly. Chinese-Vietnamese people were persecuted because of their Chinese background. Thousands of people were sent to prisons and re-education camps. The re-education camps were meant to force people to change their beliefs. Many people were also forced to work extremely hard and some people were even tortured in re-education camps.

AROUND 12 MILLION VIETNAMESE PEOPLE BECAME REFUGEES DURING THE YEARS OF THE WAR.

MOVEMENT DURING THE
VIETNAM WAR

AMERICAN SOLDIERS AND NURSES

Millions of American people were sent to Vietnam to fight as soldiers or treat wounded people as nurses. Most of the Americans lived in a large army base near Saigon, South Vietnam. The weather in Vietnam is very different to the weather in the US and many Americans found it hard to get used to the difference. Many soldiers suffered from diseases such as malaria. While some soldiers volunteered to fight in the war, many didn't want to fight. Americans in the US began to protest the war, especially as many young American soldiers were killed in battle. Many American veterans who fought in Vietnam suffer from conditions such as post-traumatic stress disorder because of what they experienced during the war.

OVER 2 MILLION AMERICANS SERVED AS SOLDIERS DURING THE WAR AND AROUND 58,000 WERE KILLED.

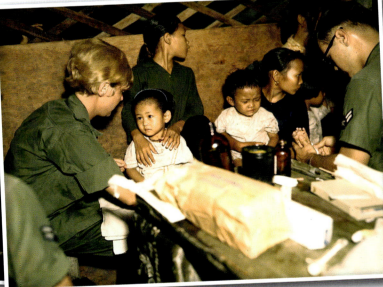

BOAT PEOPLE

The fear of persecution, torture and re-education camps forced many Vietnamese people to leave. Around 800,000 people fled Vietnam on boats. Men, women and children packed themselves onto boats and took to the sea, looking for safety in other countries around Southeast Asia. These refugees are sometimes known as the Vietnamese boat people.

DANGERS AT SEA

Sailing across the sea in boats was not safe. Many of the boats were small and overcrowded, which meant they wouldn't last on such long journeys. <u>Pirates</u> from other countries around Southeast Asia attacked the small ships to steal refugees' belongings or even kill them. Many people didn't have enough food or water to survive. Large ships from other countries often ignored the small, crowded boats, but some stopped and rescued the refugees from their small boats and brought them to land and safety. Many Vietnamese refugees who made it to land were sent to refugee camps in countries such as Malaysia, Indonesia and the US where their cases were looked at and their futures were decided.

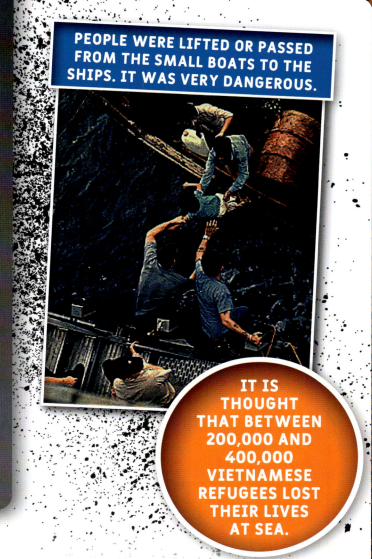

PEOPLE WERE LIFTED OR PASSED FROM THE SMALL BOATS TO THE SHIPS. IT WAS VERY DANGEROUS.

IT IS THOUGHT THAT BETWEEN 200,000 AND 400,000 VIETNAMESE REFUGEES LOST THEIR LIVES AT SEA.

RESETTLED REFUGEES

Many Vietnamese refugees found safety in different countries. Around 125,000 displaced Vietnamese refugees were resettled in the US. By 1982, around 60,000 Vietnamese refugees resettled in Australia and another 60,000 were resettled in Canada. Although many people were living with the pain the war caused, they were able to rebuild their lives. Refugees often bring their own ways of life to the areas they are resettled in. Vietnamese refugees brought their own food and culture to different countries for the first time.

TODAY, AROUND 2 MILLION VIETNAMESE-AMERICANS LIVE IN THE US.

FIND OUT MORE ABOUT REFUGEE CAMPS ON PAGE 18.

THE SYRIAN CIVIL WAR

The Syrian <u>Civil War</u> forced millions of Syrian people to leave their homes as refugees. Syrian refugees, along with refugees from other countries, were part of a 'migrant crisis' that started in 2015 in Europe. The migrant crisis got a lot of attention from the world and challenged the way governments and people view refugees and asylum seekers.

EVERYBODY HAS THE RIGHT TO EXPRESS THEMSELVES, WHICH INCLUDES BEING ABLE TO PROTEST PEACEFULLY.

In 2011, Syrian people began to protest the way the government and Syrian president, Bashar al-Assad, ruled Syria. Thousands of protestors wanted the government to change. The government began to use force and weapons to control the protests. Certain laws were changed that made it easier to arrest, imprison and even kill those who protested against the government. The violence between the government and those who were against the government worsened. Different groups began to form. Using violence, the groups began to control parts of cities and towns. By 2012, a civil war had broken out in Syria.

Certain groups used violence to gain control of areas of Syria. The violence and destruction caught the attention of countries around the world and countries such as Russia, France, the UK and the US became involved in the fighting. As well as bombing cities and towns, some groups have bombed ancient buildings and historical sites in Syria, hoping to get more power and control. People have been living in Syria for hundreds of thousands of years. The country has a rich history with many ancient buildings and treasures. Many people around the world were shocked at the treatment of Syrian people and the needless destruction that was going on in Syria.

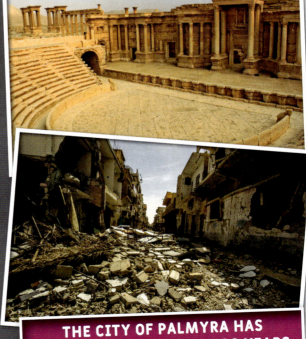

THE CITY OF PALMYRA HAS EXISTED FOR AROUND 1,800 YEARS, BUT NOW MANY OF THE OLD BUILDINGS HAVE BEEN DESTROYED.

THE USE OF WEAPONS

Both sides of the civil war used bombs and other weapons. Cities, towns, entire villages and the homes within them have been destroyed by bombing. Important buildings, such as hospitals, have also been bombed and destroyed, leaving injured people with nowhere to go. Chemical weapons are thought to have been used by both sides in the civil war, causing extreme harm to many.

MOST COUNTRIES AROUND THE WORLD HAVE AGREED NOT TO USE CHEMICAL WEAPONS. PEOPLE AROUND THE WORLD HAVE PROTESTED AGAINST THE USE OF CHEMICAL WEAPONS AND PERSECUTION AGAINST SYRIAN PEOPLE.

PERSECUTION AND DESTROYED LIVES

Many people have been tortured and killed by different groups during the civil war. If somebody disagrees with a certain group, they are often persecuted by them. Life in Syria is almost impossible for ordinary people because hospitals and schools have been destroyed in the fighting. Millions of children have had their lives changed forever by the civil war. Some children have lost their parents or been caught in the conflict themselves. Human rights are very important, and everyone's human rights deserve to be protected. However, many Syrian people's human rights are being violated because of the use of weapons and other ways they are being persecuted.

IT IS THOUGHT THAT AROUND 400,000 PEOPLE HAVE BEEN KILLED AND AROUND 10 MILLION PEOPLE HAVE BEEN DISPLACED BECAUSE OF THE SYRIAN CIVIL WAR, ALTHOUGH THESE NUMBERS COULD BE EVEN HIGHER.

MOVEMENT OF SYRIAN REFUGEES

THE JOURNEY ACROSS EUROPE

Many Syrian people had no choice but to leave the country on foot, only taking whatever they could carry with them. Travelling by foot was extremely dangerous and put many refugees at risk. There were many unexploded or abandoned bombs across Syria that refugees had to avoid. Many old, disabled or young refugees struggled to walk the journey to safety and put themselves at risk when they had to sleep in the streets at night. Traffickers and other criminals saw the refugee crisis as a way to make money, and many Syrian refugees sold their belongings to pay for transport across Europe. Many headed towards Turkey and other nearby countries, but some Syrian refugees travelled to countries such as Germany by foot, train and car. Some refugees were able to stay in Turkey in refugee camps, but many had to head to other countries to look for safety.

THOUSANDS OF MEN, WOMEN AND CHILDREN HAVE LOST THEIR LIVES TRYING TO CROSS THE MEDITERRANEAN SEA.

THE MEDITERRANEAN SEA

Many Syrian refugees have fled Syria on dinghies and boats across the Mediterranean Sea, hoping to reach the shores of countries such as Cyprus, Greece and Italy so they can seek asylum. The journey is incredibly dangerous but most people are forced to travel by boat because they can't travel in safer ways. Many Syrian refugees don't have passports, visas or other important travel documents that would allow them to fly and travel safely to a new country.

RESTRICTING MOVEMENT

Many countries across Europe have been shocked by the number of refugees seeking asylum. Although it is a human right to seek asylum and be a refugee, it is thought that some European countries have tried to control, and even <u>restrict</u>, the movement of refugees. In 2016, the <u>EU</u> made a deal with Turkey and Greece. The deal said that refugees would be held in Turkey and Greece in refugee camps, which would stop, or limit, the number of refugees entering other European countries. Many people believe that this stopped refugees from seeking asylum and violated the refugees' human rights. It is also thought that by making it harder to seek asylum, refugees are being forced into even more dangerous situations.

WAITING AT THE TURKISH <u>BORDER</u>

MANY REFUGEES HAVE REMAINED DISPLACED, WITHOUT ACCESS TO PROPER SHELTER OR FOOD, WHILE THEY WAIT AT COUNTRY BORDERS OR IN REFUGEE CAMPS FOR ASYLUM.

MANY SYRIAN REFUGEES WANT TO RETURN TO SYRIA AND THEIR HOMES, BUT CAN'T BECAUSE THEIR HOMES AND COMMUNITIES HAVE BEEN DESTROYED.

REACTIONS TO REFUGEES

There have been many reactions to the movement of Syrian refugees across the world. Some people don't know about or understand the Syrian Civil War and think that countries shouldn't give asylum or help Syrian refugees. Other people believe that their governments shouldn't spend lots of money helping refugees when people in their own countries need help. The way that the <u>media</u> around the world shows Syrian refugees can also have an effect on the way people react to refugees. Charities, organisations and many people around the world try to help Syrian refugees. Many people protest in their countries to try and help refugees and change the way their governments act.

REFUGEE CAMPS

WHAT IS A REFUGEE CAMP?

A refugee camp is a <u>temporary</u> shelter for displaced refugees to live in. Many refugees travel to, or get sent to, refugee camps when they reach a new country. This is because refugees usually aren't allowed to live in a new country straight away. Refugees can apply for asylum in the country the refugee camp is in or a nearby country. Refugees who have applied for asylum become known as asylum seekers. They are usually not allowed to leave the camp until they are given asylum. Some asylum seekers can spend years of their life in a refugee camp waiting to be given asylum.

REFUGEES IN THIS SOMALIAN REFUGEE CAMP LIVED IN TENTS.

EVERY CHILD HAS THE RIGHT TO GROW UP IN A SAFE PLACE WITH THEIR FAMILY AND GO TO SCHOOL, BUT OVER 3 MILLION REFUGEE CHILDREN AROUND THE WORLD DON'T GO TO SCHOOL.

LIFE IN A REFUGEE CAMP

Although most refugee camps don't have the infrastructure that a city or town has, many of them exist for years. Some refugee camps become communities that have services such as schools or hospitals. However, most refugee camps are extremely overcrowded and don't have enough food or water for everybody there. Many people become sick and can't get proper treatment. Living in a refugee camp can be dangerous as lots of people are cramped together without proper security. <u>Orphan</u> children and those who have been separated from their family are extremely <u>vulnerable</u>.

REFUGEE CAMPS IN GUAM

Many refugee camps are set up by different governments or charities. In 1975, the US government ran missions to rescue Vietnamese refugees. Vietnamese refugees were <u>evacuated</u> by American ships and planes and brought to refugee camps that were set up by the American government. There were more than ten refugee camps on the US island Guam in the Pacific Ocean. Vietnamese refugees were brought to refugee camps while they waited to get permission to resettle in the US. The refugee camps struggled with overcrowding; 30-40 people were living in each tent, but American nurses managed to help and treat many refugees.

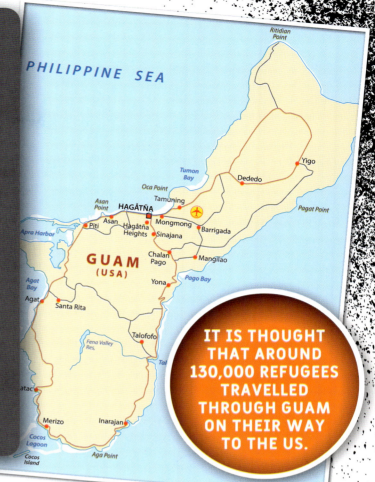

IT IS THOUGHT THAT AROUND 130,000 REFUGEES TRAVELLED THROUGH GUAM ON THEIR WAY TO THE US.

THE JUNGLE

Refugees who were trying to enter countries such as the UK and France lived in the Jungle, a refugee camp in Calais, France. Refugees had been coming to Calais since 1999 because they could apply for asylum in countries such as France and the UK. In 2014, the number of refugees in the Jungle began to grow as refugees from Syria, Somalia and Eritrea were forced to leave their homes and travel across Europe to look for safety. The Jungle became a crowded, unclean and dangerous place to live. Many refugees lived in shipping containers and some lived in tents. In 2016, the French government decided that the Jungle was not a safe place for refugees to live and destroyed it. While the French government helped to move many refugees, some believe that by destroying the Jungle, many vulnerable refugees have been put in more danger.

SHIPPING CONTAINERS

THE JUNGLE DID NOT GET SUPPORT FROM GOVERNMENTS AND RELIED ON CHARITIES AND VOLUNTEERS FOR HELP.

LIFE AS A REFUGEE

APPLYING FOR ASYLUM

Many countries around the world have special systems in place that a refugee must follow when they apply for asylum. In some countries, such as the UK, refugees can travel to the country and apply for asylum when they get there. In other countries, refugees have to apply for asylum before they enter the country from a refugee camp. Asylum seekers have to go to special interviews where they must prove their human rights are being violated and that they fear going back to their home country. Asylum seekers are usually given somewhere to live by the government. Some asylum seekers have to wait months before a decision is made. If the government accepts their claims for asylum, the asylum seeker will be given refugee status and permission to stay in the country for a certain amount of time.

ASYLUM SEEKERS MUST TELL BORDER CONTROL THAT THEY WANT TO CLAIM ASYLUM FROM THE UK WHEN THEY ENTER THE COUNTRY.

AN ASYLUM SEEKER IN THE UK IS GIVEN £37.75 PER WEEK TO LIVE OFF. ASYLUM SEEKERS IN THE UK ARE ONLY ALLOWED TO GET A JOB IF THEY HAVE BEEN IN THE UK FOR MORE THAN 12 MONTHS AND ARE STILL WAITING FOR THE GOVERNMENT TO MAKE A DECISION. MANY OTHER COUNTRIES ALLOW ASYLUM SEEKERS TO GET JOBS.

REFUGEE LIFE

When somebody becomes a refugee in the UK, they have 28 days to find their own place to live. When an asylum seeker is given refugee status, they are usually able to start working and most refugees are able to open a bank account for the first time. Many refugees find it difficult to get a job, even if they are trained or have special skills. This can be upsetting as many refugees want to give back, or help the places that have helped them. Refugees are also allowed to bring their close family to the new country to live in safety.

A NEW LIFE

Living in a new country can be scary, especially if you don't speak the language. Many asylum seekers and refugees find it hard to get used to living in a new country because there can be many differences in the cultures and ways of life. Simple things, such as going to the doctor or buying food in a supermarket, can be very difficult for some refugees. It takes time for people to get used to living in a new place, but different people can share their cultures and learn from each other.

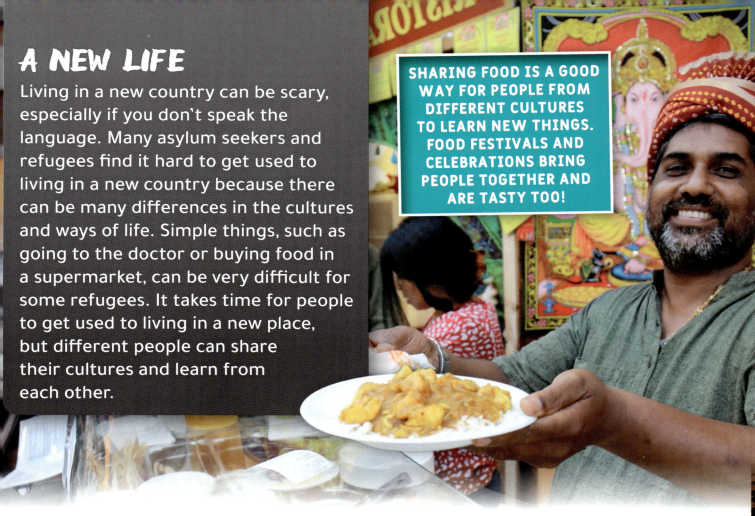

SHARING FOOD IS A GOOD WAY FOR PEOPLE FROM DIFFERENT CULTURES TO LEARN NEW THINGS. FOOD FESTIVALS AND CELEBRATIONS BRING PEOPLE TOGETHER AND ARE TASTY TOO!

LEARNING AND GROWING

Re-integration charities help refugees and asylum seekers get used to living in a new country. Some refugees might not have the skills they need to work or get by because their lives have been interrupted. Many charities help refugees by helping them to learn a new language and any skills that they might need when they start working. Without the support from charities and volunteers, some asylum seekers and refugees may struggle.

REFUGEE WEEK IS CELEBRATED ONCE A YEAR IN THE UK AND AIMS TO SHARE THE STORIES AND EXPERIENCES OF REFUGEES.

RE-INTEGRATION MEANS HELPING SOMEBODY FIT IN TO A COMMUNITY.

DISPLACEMENT

WHAT IS DISPLACEMENT?

Displacement is when a person has been forced to move from their usual home and stop doing the things they usually do. For example, a displaced person can't live in their usual home or go to their usual job.

REFUGEES ARE OFTEN DESCRIBED AS DISPLACED PEOPLE BECAUSE THEY HAVE BEEN FORCED TO LEAVE THEIR HOMES.

INTERNALLY DISPLACED

An internally displaced person is somebody who has been forced to leave their usual home and is still in their home country. It can be hard for internally displaced people to get help from other countries because they haven't left their home country and crossed a border like a refugee. They are not thought of as refugees by the law and the Refugee Convention.

OVER 1.5 MILLION PEOPLE HAVE BECOME INTERNALLY DISPLACED IN SOMALIA BECAUSE OF FIGHTING, DROUGHT AND FLOODING.

An internally displaced person may have left their home and found shelter in a nearby city, town or refugee camp. Internally displaced people have to get help from their own government, but this isn't always possible. Some internally displaced people could be displaced because of fighting caused by their own government, or their government might not be able to afford to help internally displaced people.

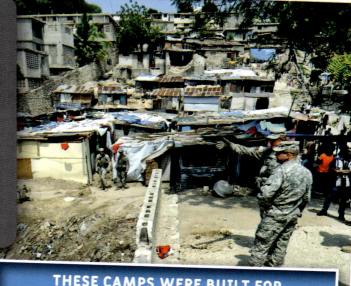

DISASTER DISPLACEMENT

The causes of displacement are similar to those that make someone a refugee. Many people are displaced because of natural disasters. Natural disasters such as flooding, earthquakes, tsunamis and hurricanes can damage communities and their infrastructure. This makes it impossible for people to go about their daily lives safely, displacing people and forcing them to look for help. There will always be natural disasters, so it is important for countries and governments to be ready to help people displaced by them.

THOUSANDS OF FOREST FIRES HAPPEN IN AUSTRALIA EVERY YEAR, DISPLACING MANY PEOPLE.

2004 INDIAN OCEAN EARTHQUAKE AND
TSUNAMI

The 2004 Indian Ocean earthquake and tsunami was a terrible natural disaster that displaced over 1 million people. Let's take a look at what happened and how it forced people to move.

WHAT IS A TSUNAMI?

A tsunami is usually caused by a large underwater earthquake or underwater volcanic eruption. The force of the earthquake or volcanic eruption creates multiple waves in the sea. The waves get bigger as they travel outwards from the centre of the earthquake and cause damage when they reach land.

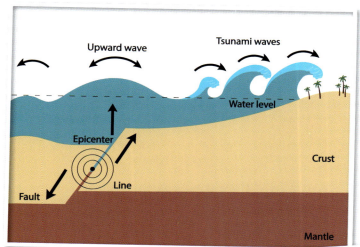

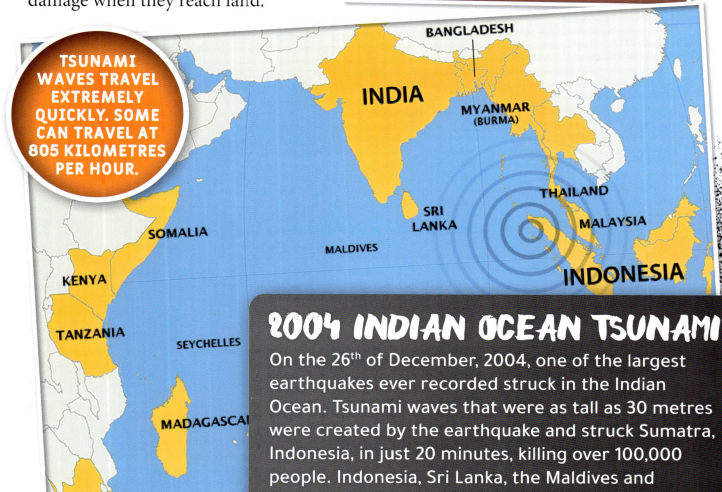

TSUNAMI WAVES TRAVEL EXTREMELY QUICKLY. SOME CAN TRAVEL AT 805 KILOMETRES PER HOUR.

2004 INDIAN OCEAN TSUNAMI

On the 26th of December, 2004, one of the largest earthquakes ever recorded struck in the Indian Ocean. Tsunami waves that were as tall as 30 metres were created by the earthquake and struck Sumatra, Indonesia, in just 20 minutes, killing over 100,000 people. Indonesia, Sri Lanka, the Maldives and Thailand were badly affected. The tsunami waves travelled 8,000 kilometres and affected countries as far away as South Africa.

NO WARNING

While there was a way to detect the earthquake and tsunami, there weren't proper ways of letting different countries know that the tsunami was coming. Millions of people weren't told to evacuate or find safety.

THE RICHTER SCALE MEASURES HOW STRONG AN EARTHQUAKE IS. THE EARTHQUAKE THAT CAUSED THE TSUNAMI MEASURED 9.1 ON THE RICHTER SCALE AND IS ONE OF THE STRONGEST EARTHQUAKES RECORDED.

DESTRUCTION

A tsunami wave can start off being 30 centimetres high but grow to 30 metres high by the time it reaches the shore. As the tsunami waves get bigger, they are more powerful. There are usually multiple tsunami waves that reach the shore one after the other. 18 countries were affected by the tsunami. Tsunami waves smash into buildings, trees and cars, destroying the infrastructure of cities and towns and everything in their path. Even if the waves aren't big enough to destroy things, the tsunami waves can cause floods and can sweep away boats and cars.

1.0-1.9
2.0-2.9
3.0-3.9
4.0-4.9
5.0-5.9
6.0-6.9
7.0-7.9
8.0-8.9
9.0 AND GREATER

LARGE PARTS OF THE COASTAL CITY BANDA ACEH IN INDONESIA WERE DESTROYED BY THE TSUNAMI.

AROUND 230,000 PEOPLE LOST THEIR LIVES AND 1.7 MILLION PEOPLE WERE DISPLACED BECAUSE OF THE TSUNAMI.

MOVEMENT OF PEOPLE AFTER THE
TSUNAMI

REFUGEE CAMPS

Many people lost their homes and became internally displaced after the tsunami. The tsunami also destroyed the infrastructure of many communities, causing more problems. Many countries set up refugee camps, or relief camps, so internally displaced people could move into temporary shelters. It took a long time for permanent houses to be rebuilt so many people lived in refugee camps for longer than expected. Some displaced people took shelter in local schools and religious buildings. It was important to move displaced people to refugee camps or other safe areas after the tsunami.

140,000 NEW HOMES WERE BUILT IN INDONESIA AFTER THE TSUNAMI.

The tsunami has had long-lasting effects on people's lives. As well as losing their homes, many displaced people couldn't work. Farmers and fishermen were badly affected. The tsunami had brought in waves of seawater. The salty seawater destroyed farmland and made the farmland so salty that plants and crops couldn't be grown. Fishermen couldn't work because the tsunami destroyed their boats. While some governments were able to give money to those who couldn't work, many people struggled.

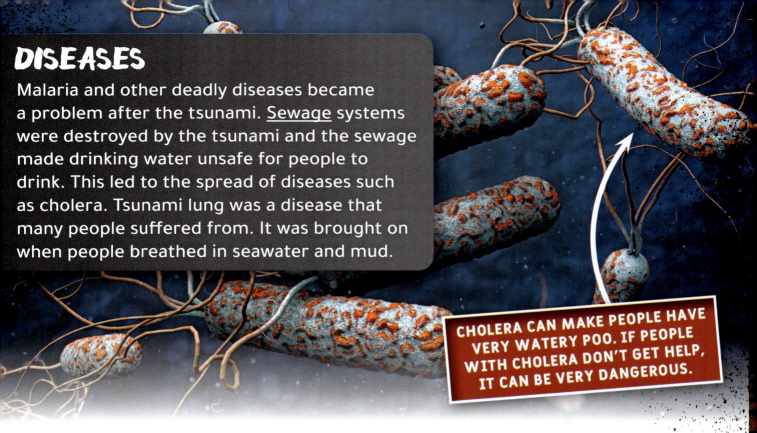

DISEASES

Malaria and other deadly diseases became a problem after the tsunami. Sewage systems were destroyed by the tsunami and the sewage made drinking water unsafe for people to drink. This led to the spread of diseases such as cholera. Tsunami lung was a disease that many people suffered from. It was brought on when people breathed in seawater and mud.

CHOLERA CAN MAKE PEOPLE HAVE VERY WATERY POO. IF PEOPLE WITH CHOLERA DON'T GET HELP, IT CAN BE VERY DANGEROUS.

PROVIDING AID

Many other countries and charities around the world offered to help, or aid, the areas badly affected by the tsunami. Aid workers and volunteers from other countries were sent to the affected areas to help support displaced people and bring important supplies such as medicine, food and water to those who needed it. Aid is extremely important and needed to help stop diseases and illnesses from spreading.

HURRICANE
KATRINA

Hurricane Katrina was a natural disaster that displaced many people. It also raised important questions about how countries can be prepared for natural disasters.

WHAT IS A HURRICANE?

A hurricane is a type of storm. Hurricanes form when warm air near the ocean rises and spins in a circle. When the warm air gets high enough, it cools down and forms spinning clouds. Warm air carries on rising up and the clouds get bigger and bigger and a dangerous storm, or hurricane, forms.

HURRICANE KATRINA

Hurricane Katrina was a storm that formed off the east coast of Florida in the US. It became one of the most powerful hurricanes to have ever happened in the area. It reached land on the 25th of August, 2005, sweeping over Florida. It then moved across the Gulf of Mexico and became an even stronger hurricane. At its strongest, the winds reached a speed of over 275 kilometres per hour.

LOUISIANA

MISSISSIPPI

NEW ORLEANS

GULF OF MEXICO

FLORIDA

MIAMI

EVACUATION

The areas in Hurricane Katrina's path took steps before the hurricane reached them, and many people started to evacuate the areas and head to safety. However, there were many problems. Local governments had asked for buses to help evacuate people, but there weren't enough buses for everybody, and many people couldn't afford the bus tickets. This forced some people to remain in their homes without proper shelter. The government failed to send buses to vulnerable people in <u>nursing homes</u>, and many people in nursing homes were made to wait for the storm to pass before being moved somewhere safe. Some people who made it on the buses were separated from their families during the journey to shelter.

ROADS AND WAYS OUT OF CITIES ARE USUALLY BLOCKED BY TRAFFIC AS EVERYONE TRIES TO EVACUATE.

SHELTER

People who couldn't evacuate from cities such as New Orleans and Houston were given shelter in refugee camps. Sports stadiums were used as temporary shelters for thousands of people. While they offered temporary shelter, conditions inside the stadiums were unclean and cramped. Many people stayed in the Superdome in New Orleans. They were safe there until the city's flood defences broke and New Orleans flooded. A lot of people were angry that the government didn't prepare properly and failed to protect so many people.

MANY PEOPLE FROM THE SUPERDOME WERE MOVED TO THE ASTRODOME IN HOUSTON, TEXAS.

THINGS TO THINK ABOUT

Sometimes it can be tricky to understand what's happening in the world. It's important to talk to lots of different people about the world. We can learn a lot by sharing our experiences and listening to other people's stories. Try talking about the following questions with your family and friends. Remember, it might be difficult for somebody to talk about any bad experiences they have had. Try and understand if somebody doesn't want to talk about their experiences.

- Where does your family come from?
- Have you ever moved school, house or country? How did you feel about moving?
- How would you feel if you were made to move away from your home?

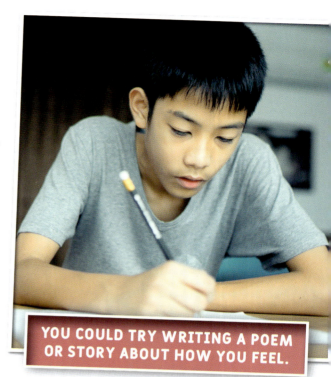

YOU COULD TRY WRITING A POEM OR STORY ABOUT HOW YOU FEEL.

HOW TO HELP

There are plenty of ways to help refugees. You could visit a local refugee charity and offer to help or make a donation. You could also find out if your school is a school of sanctuary. Schools of sanctuary teach people the importance of safety for everybody. You could also check if your local area celebrates Refugee Week. Refugee Week celebrates refugees and helps to bring people in a community together.

DONATE

GLOSSARY

asylum protection given to somebody by a state or government

border the line between different countries

chemical weapons weapons that use gases and other chemicals to cause harm to other people

civil war a war between different groups in the same country

dinghies small boats that are usually used for short journeys

EU the European Union, a group of countries in Europe

evacuated to have left a place in order to be safe

famine when large numbers of people do not have enough food

government the group of people with the power to run a country and decide its laws

herbicides chemicals that are used to kill plants

house arrest when a person isn't allowed to leave their house as a punishment

infrastructure the basic services, such as a power supply and roads, that a community needs in order to function

media the different ways that information is shown to the public, such as TV, adverts, newspapers and radio

natural disasters natural events, such as earthquakes or floods, that cause serious damage and loss of life

nursing homes places where elderly or sick people are cared for

orphan a child who does not have any parents

permanently lasting forever

persecution cruel or unfair treatment based on religion, political beliefs, where a person is from or what they look like

pirates people who attack and rob ships at sea

political systems the ways that governments and leaders rule a country

post-traumatic stress disorder a condition that is caused by extremely stressful events

protest an action that shows disagreement with something

restrict to limit or put things in place that stop something happening

rights things that a person can have or do because of the law

sewage wastewater from homes and factories that often includes human waste

status a person's position and situation at a particular time, to do with moving to new countries

temporary lasting for a short time

tortured to have deliberately caused great pain to a person or animal

traffickers people who trade things, and sometimes people, illegally

UN stands for United Nations, an organisation that formed after World War Two that is made up of countries around the world

veterans people who have fought during a war

violated to have broken or failed to keep

visas when permissions have been given for a person to visit a certain country or stay for a certain amount of time

volunteered to have done work or helped for free

vote to choose who runs or rules an area

vulnerable when someone is more likely to get into danger or be hurt, attacked or injured

well-founded based on good reasons

INDEX